CONTENTS 1B

I'm Happy

Learn

Words

A Listen and repeat. Then chant. 03 04

B Listen and repeat. 05

C Stick and say.

I'm happy.

1 happy

2 sad

3 angry

4 scared

5 sleepy

6 hungry

7 thirsty

8 sick

Quiz

Listen, find, and draw. 🎧06

1 ◯ **2** △ **3** ☐

Let's Listen

A Listen and sing. Then match.

I'm Happy

I'm sad. I'm sad.

I'm angry. I'm angry.

I'm scared. I'm scared.

I'm happy. I'm happy.

B Listen and stick. Then say.

Let's Talk

Listen and number. Then say. 🎧09

sick ◯

I'm _____.

thirsty ◯

hungry ◯

happy ◯

sad ◯

sleepy ◯

Words

A Match and trace.

1

2

3

4

sick	thirsty	hungry	happy
sad	sleepy	angry	scared

5

6

7

8

Subject Link

sick   happy
sad   scared

A Write and say.

1

I'm _____.

2

I'm _____.

3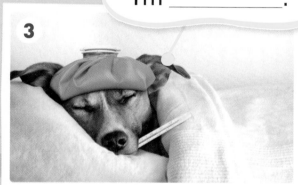

I'm _____.

4

I'm _____.

B How do you feel? Draw and write.

I'm _____.

A Listen and number. 🎧 10

B Listen and circle. 🎧 11

1	sad	sick

2	scared	sleepy

3	angry	thirsty

4	happy	hungry

C Listen and choose. Then say. 🎧 12

1

2

Phonics

Ⓐ Listen, say, and write. 🎧 13

`a + d → ad`

1 s**ad**   d☐☐   b☐☐

`a + n → an`

2  c**an**   p☐☐   f☐☐

Ⓑ Listen and match. 🎧 14

1   d

2   c

3   s

4   p

 -ad   -an

Ⓒ Look and write.

1  d_____

2  c_____

3  b_____

4  p_____

UNIT 2 I Have a Dog

Learn

Words

Ⓐ Listen and repeat. Then chant. ▶ 🎧16 🎧17

Ⓑ Listen and repeat. ▶ 🎧18

Ⓒ Stick and say.

I have a dog.

1 dog

2 cat

3 rabbit

4 pig

10

5 fish

6 parrot

7 hamster

8 turtle

Quiz

Listen, find, and draw. 🎧19

1 ◯   2 △   3 ▢

Let's Listen

A Listen and sing. Then match. ▶ 🎧20

I Have a Pet

Dog, I have a dog.

Cat, I have a cat.

Rabbit, I have a rabbit.

Pig, I have a pig.

B Listen and match. Then say. 🎧21

1

2

3

4

Let's Talk

A Listen and stick. Then say. 🎧 22

2 TURTLE

3 DOG

1 CAT

4 FISH

5 HAMSTER

6 PARROT

I have a _____ .

Words

Ⓐ **Look and write.**

cat	dog	rabbit	parrot
pig	turtle	hamster	fish

Subject Link

rabbit   turtle
fish   dog

A Write and say.

1

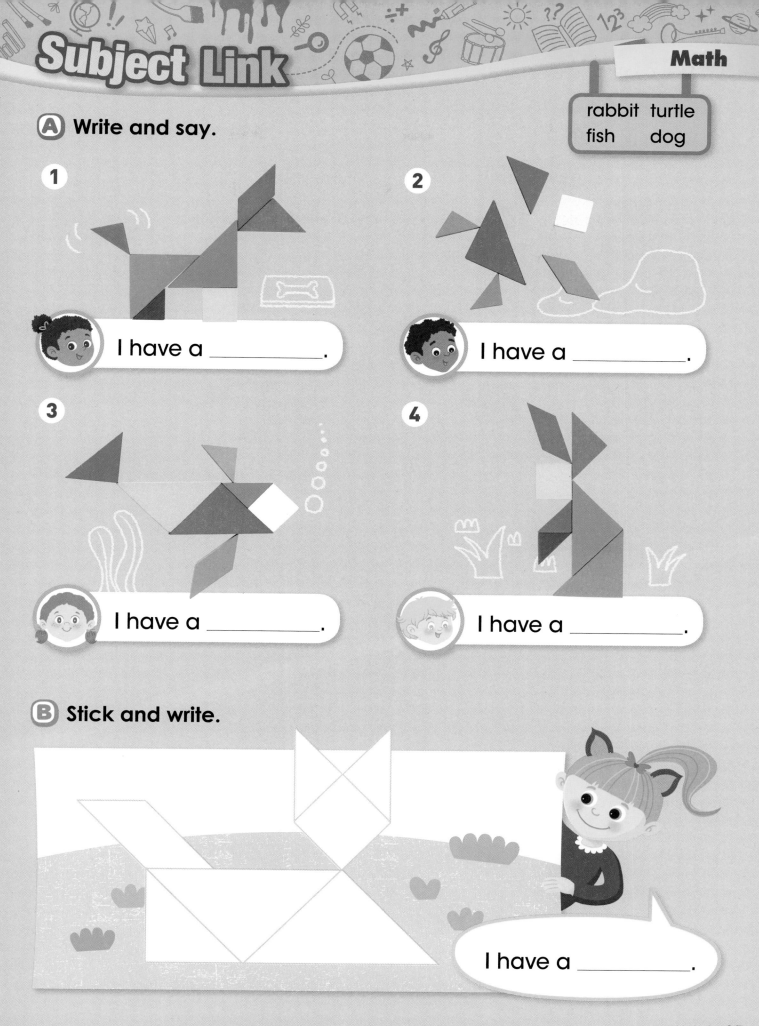

I have a _____.

2

I have a _____.

3

I have a _____.

4

I have a _____.

B Stick and write.

I have a _____.

A Listen and check. 🎧23

1

2

3

4

B Listen and number. 🎧24

| rabbit | dog | pig | turtle |

C Listen and choose. Then say. 🎧25

1
a
b

2
a
b

Phonics

A Listen, say, and write. 🎧26

a + p → ap

 1 cap

 m ☐☐

 t ☐☐

a + t → at

2  cat

b ☐☐

 h ☐☐

B Listen and circle. 🎧27

1 c _____ _____   -ap -at

2 c _____ _____   -ap -at

3 h _____ _____   -ap -at

4 m _____ _____   -ap -at

C Circle and write.

1

-ap -at

b _____

2

-ap -at

m _____

3

-ap -at

h _____

A Listen and number. 28

B **Read and check.**

1

☐ I'm hungry.
☐ I'm sleepy.

2

☐ I have a dog.
☐ I have a parrot.

3

☐ I'm angry.
☐ I'm thirsty.

4

☐ I have a cat.
☐ I have a hamster.

5

☐ I'm sad.
☐ I'm scared.

6

☐ I have a fish.
☐ I have a turtle.

I Can Jump

Learn

Words
A Listen and repeat. Then chant. ▶ 🎧30 🎧31

B Listen and repeat. ▶ 🎧32

C Stick and say.

I can jump.

1 jump

2 sing

3 climb

4 run

Let's Talk

Words

A Circle and write.

1
swim
sing
jump

_____

2
climb
sing
walk

_____

3
fly
run
climb

_____

4
fly
run
dance

_____

5
jump
walk
swim

_____

6
swim
walk
climb

_____

7
fly
run
dance

_____

8
jump
dance
sing

_____

Subject Link

run   swim
jump   dance

A Write and say.

1

I can _____.

2

I can _____.

3

I can _____.

4

I can _____.

B Choose and write.

I can _____.

Check-Up

A Listen and match. 🎧37

B Listen and check. 🎧38

1	swim	run		2	jump	sing
	☐	☐			☐	☐

3	dance	walk		4	climb	fly
	☐	☐			☐	☐

C Listen and choose. Then say. 🎧39

1  ⓐ ⓑ

2  ⓐ ⓑ

Phonics

A Listen, say, and write. 🎧 40

`i + g → ig`

 p**ig**

 b☐☐

 w☐☐

`i + x → ix`

2

 s**ix**

 m☐☐

 f☐☐

B Listen and match. 🎧 41

1

2

3

4

-ig

-ix

C Look and write.

1

f_____

2

b_____

3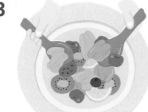

m_____

UNIT 4 Touch Your Nose

Learn

Words

A Listen and repeat. Then chant. ▶

B Listen and repeat. ▶ 🎧 45

C Stick and say.

Touch your nose.

1 eyes

2 nose

3 ears

4 mouth

5 head

6 arms

7 legs

8 feet

Listen, find, and draw. 🎧46

1 ◯ **2** △ **3** ☐

Let's Listen

A Listen and sing. Then match. ▶ 🎧47

Touch Your Eyes

Touch your eyes. (Eyes!)

Touch your nose. Nose!

Touch your mouth. Mouth!

Touch your ears. Ears!

B Listen and circle. 🎧48

1
2
3
4

Let's Talk

Listen and number. Then say. 49

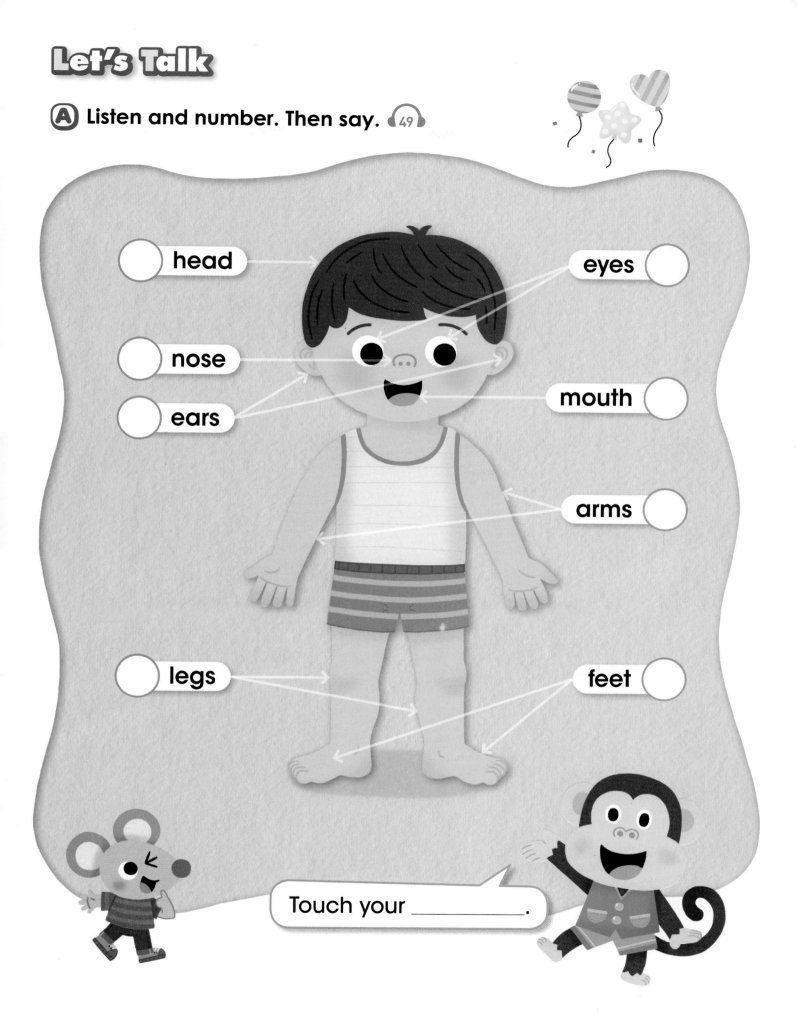

head

nose

ears

legs

eyes

mouth

arms

feet

Touch your _____.

Words

A Trace and circle.

1 arms
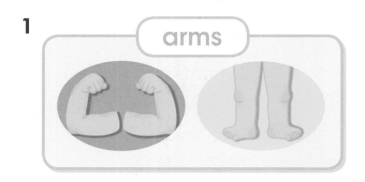

2 ears
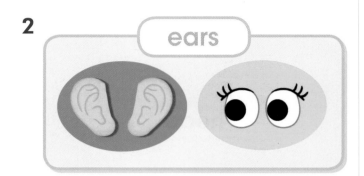

3 mouth
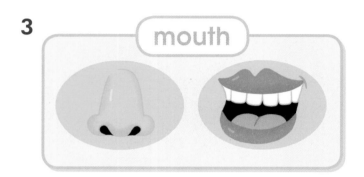

4 feet

5 legs
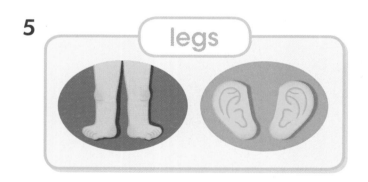

6 eyes
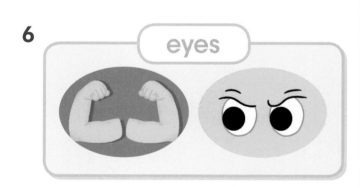

7 head

8 nose
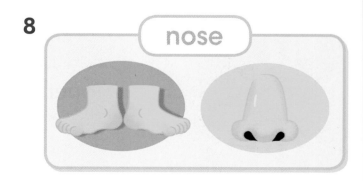

Subject Link

arms legs
head feet

A Write and say.

1

Touch your _____.

2

Touch your _____.

3

Touch your _____.

4

Touch your _____.

B Stick and write.

Touch your _____.

Check-Up

A Listen and number. 🎧50

B Listen and match. 🎧51

1	2	3	4

mouth	nose	feet	arms

C Listen and choose. Then say. 🎧52

1

2

Phonics

A Listen, say, and write. 🎧 53

i + n → in

1
 p**in**

 f☐☐

 w☐☐

i + t → it

2
 s**it**

 h☐☐

 f☐☐

B Listen and circle. 🎧 54

1
| sit | sad | six |

2
| pig | pin | pan |

3
| hit | fit | hat |

4
| fan | fix | fin |

C Circle and write.

1

-in   -it

p _____

2

-in   -it

w _____

3

-in   -it

s _____

A Listen and number. 🎧 55

Ⓑ **Read and circle.**

I can
dance
sing
.

Touch your
feet
ears
.

I can
climb
fly
.

Touch your
eyes
arms
.

I can
run
swim
.

Touch your
nose
head
.

UNIT 5 It's Sunny

Learn

Words

(A) Listen and repeat. Then chant.  57 58

(B) Listen and repeat. 59

(C) Stick and say.

It's sunny.

1 sunny

2 cloudy

3 windy

38

4 hot

5 cold

6 rainy

7 snowy

Listen, find, and draw. 🎧60

1 ◯ **2** △ **3** ▢

Let's Listen

A Listen and sing. Then match. 61

It's Sunny

Sunny, sunny. It's sunny.

Cloudy, cloudy. It's cloudy.

Rainy, rainy. It's rainy.

Snowy, snowy. It's snowy.

B Listen and stick. Then say. 62

❶ Sticker

❷ Sticker

❸ Sticker

❹ Sticker

Let's Talk

Listen and connect. Then say. 63

It's _____.

1 sunny

2 rainy

3 cold

4 windy

5 hot

6 snowy

Words

A Look and write.

1
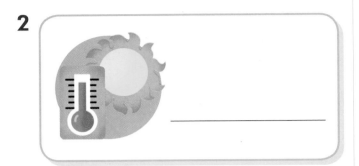
_____

2

_____

3

_____

4

_____

5

_____

6
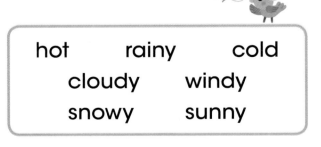
_____

7
_____

hot   rainy   cold
cloudy   windy
snowy   sunny

Subject Link

snowy hot
windy rainy

(A) Stick, write, and say.

1

It's _____.

2

It's _____.

3

It's _____.

4

It's _____.

(B) How's the weather today? Draw and write.

It's _____.

Check-Up

A Listen and number. 🎧64

B Listen and check. 🎧65

1	snowy	rainy
	☐	☐

2	sunny	cloudy
	☐	☐

3	hot	cold
	☐	☐

4	windy	rainy
	☐	☐

C Listen and choose. Then say. 🎧66

1
ⓐ ⓑ

2
ⓐ ⓑ

A Listen, say, and write.

o + t → ot   o + p → op   o + x → ox

1

hot   p [ ][ ]

2

top   m [ ][ ]

3

box   f [ ][ ]

B Listen and match.

1   p
2   t
3   b
4   f

-op   -ot   -ox

C Circle and write.

1

-at -ot

2

-ix -ox

3

-op -ot

_____   _____   _____

Put on Your Skirt

Learn

Words
A Listen and repeat. Then chant. ▶ 70 71

B Listen and repeat. ▶ 72

C Stick and say.

Put on your skirt.

1 dress

2 skirt

3 jacket

4 socks

5 shorts

6 pants

7 T-shirt

8 cap

Quiz

Listen, find, and draw. 73

1 ○ **2** △ **3** □

Let's Listen

A Listen and sing. Then match.

Put on Your T-shirt

Put on your T-shirt.

T-shirt!

Put on your pants. Pants!

Put on your skirt. Skirt!

Put on your dress. Dress!

B Listen and number. Then say.

Let's Talk

Put on your _____.

Words

A Trace and match.

1 T-shirt

2 cap

3 skirt

4 pants

5 shorts

6 jacket

7 dress

8 socks

Subject Link

socks jacket
dress pants

A Stick, write, and say.

Put on your
_____ .

Put on your
_____ .

Put on your
_____ .

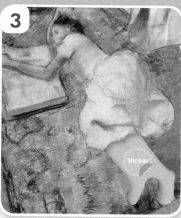

Put on your
_____ .

B Draw and write.

Put on your _____ .

Check-Up

A Listen and match. 🎧 77

1   2   3   4

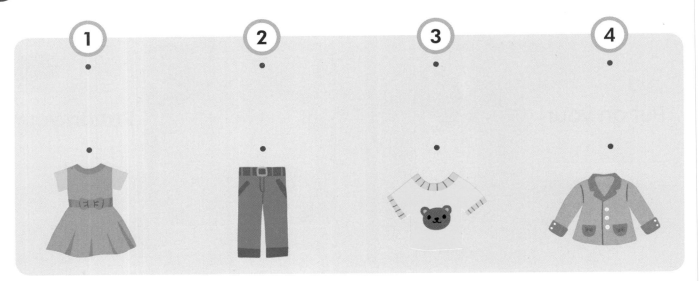

B Listen and mark ○ or ✕. 🎧 78

1   socks

2   T-shirt

3   cap

4   pants

C Listen and choose. Then say. 🎧 79

1

ⓐ ⓑ

2

ⓐ ⓑ

Phonics

A Listen, say, and write. 🎧 80

u + n → un

1
 r**un**

 s ⬜⬜

 f ⬜⬜

u + t → ut

2
 n**ut**

 h ⬜⬜

 c ⬜⬜

B Listen and choose. 🎧 81

1 r _____ _____   -ut -un

2 c _____ _____   -un -ut

3 f _____ _____   -un -ut

4 h _____ _____   -ut -un

C Look and write.

1

s_____

2

r_____

3

c_____

Review 3

A Listen and number. 82

B Read and match.

1 It's windy.

3 It's rainy.

2 It's hot.

4 It's cold.

5 Put on your skirt.

7 Put on your shorts.

6 Put on your socks.

8 Put on your jacket.

I See a Plane

Learn

Words
A Listen and repeat. Then chant.
B Listen and repeat. 86
C Stick and say.

What do you see?

I see a plane.

1 plane

2 car

TAXI

3 taxi

4 ship

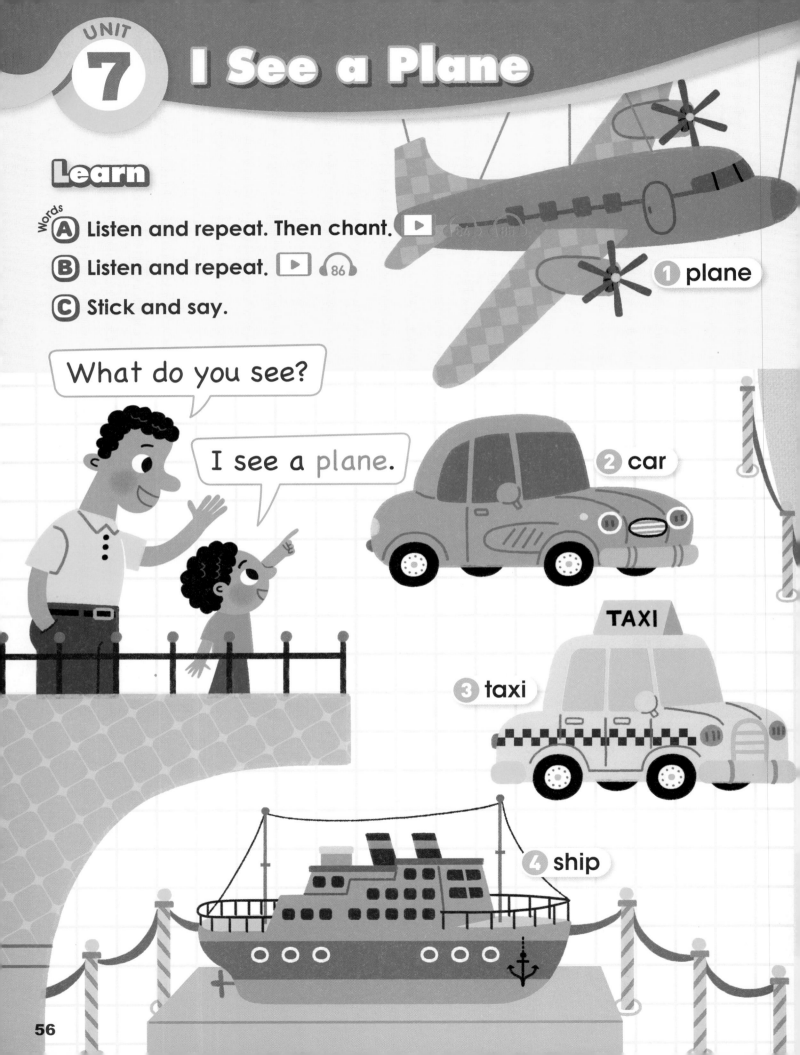

6 train

5 bike

7 bus

8 truck

Quiz

Listen, find, and draw. 🎧87

1 ◯ **2** △ **3** ▢

Let's Listen

A Listen and sing. Then match. 88

I See a Plane

What do you see?

Plane, plane. I see a plane.

Bus, bus. I see a bus.

Car, car. I see a car.

Truck, truck. I see a truck.

B Listen and match. Then ask and answer. 89

1

2

3

4

Let's Talk

(A) Listen and stick. Then ask and answer.

What do you see?

I see a _____.

1 train

2 plane

3 taxi

4 bus

5 ship

6 bike

Words

A Circle and write.

1

bus
car

_____

2

ship
train

_____

3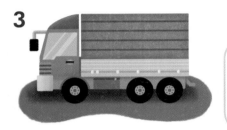

truck
taxi

_____

4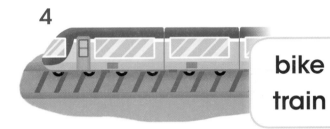

bike
train

_____

5

car
plane

_____

6

bike
ship

_____

7

taxi
truck

_____

8

plane
bus

_____

Subject Link

car   train
ship   plane

A Write and say.

1

I see a _____.

2

I see a _____.

3

I see a _____.

4

I see a _____.

B What do you see? Color and write.

I see a _____.

Check-Up

A Listen and number. 🎧91

☐   ☐   ☐   ☐

B Listen and match. 🎧92

① ② ③ ④

•   •   •   •

•   •   •   •

taxi   ship   plane   train

C Listen and choose. Then ask and answer. 🎧93

1

2

ⓐ ⓑ   ⓐ ⓑ

A Listen, say, and write.  94

u + g → ug   u + b → ub   u + p → up

1

bug   h☐☐

2

t**ub**   c☐☐

3

up   c☐☐

B Listen and circle. 95

1
| bug | hug | big |

2
| cub | tub | cup |

3
| hat | hut | hug |

4
| cut | cup | tap |

C Match and write.

1  •

2  •

3  •

• b •   • -up _____

• c •   • -ub _____

• t •   • -ug _____

I Want an Apple

Learn

Words

A Listen and repeat. Then chant. ▶ 🎧97 🎧98

B Listen and repeat. ▶ 🎧99

C Stick and say.

What do you want?

1 a banana

2 an orange   3 an apple

I want an apple.

4 a kiwi
5 a mango
6 a carrot
7 a potato
8 an onion

I want a kiwi.

Quiz

Listen, find, and draw. 🎧100

1 ◯ 2 △ 3 ▢

Let's Listen

A Listen and sing. Then match. ▶ 🎧101

I Want an Apple

What do you want?

I want an apple. An apple.

I want an onion. An onion.

I want a carrot. A carrot.

I want a kiwi. A kiwi.

B Listen and number. Then draw. 🎧102

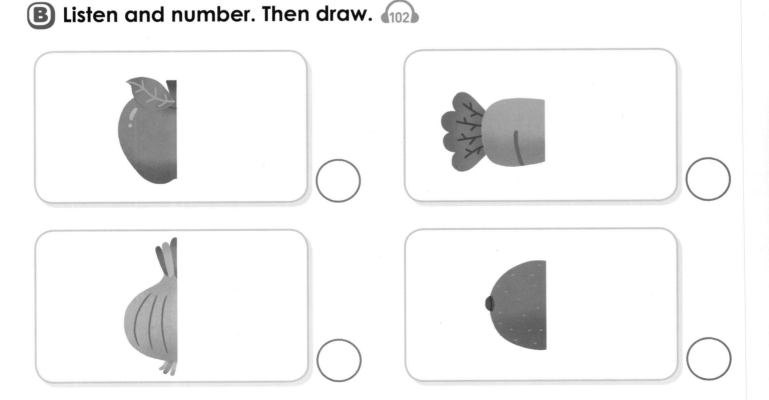

Let's Talk

A Listen and match. Then ask and answer. 103

Words

A Match and trace.

1

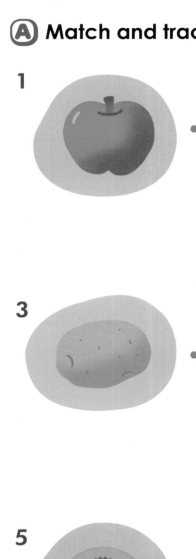

2

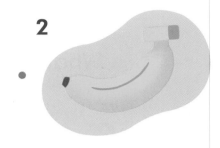

 potato

 onion

3

kiwi

4

banana

5

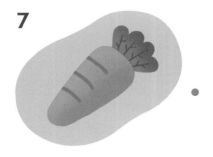

apple

6

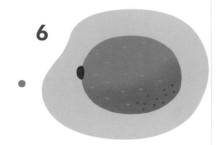

 mango

orange

7

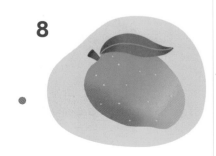

8

 carrot

Subject Link

kiwi   apple
onion carrot

A Write and stick.

1

I want an _____.

2

I want an _____.

3

I want a _____.

4

I want a _____.

B Color and write.

I want an _____.

Unit 8 **69**

A Listen and check. 🎧104

1

2

3
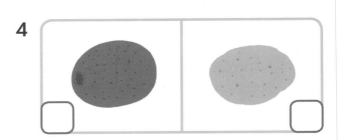

4

B Listen and number. 🎧105

orange	banana	carrot	potato
◯	◯	◯	◯

C Listen and choose. Then ask and answer. 🎧106

1

ⓐ

ⓑ

2

ⓐ

ⓑ

Phonics

(A) Listen, say, and write. 🎧 107

1

bed r ☐☐

2

pen t ☐☐

3

jet w ☐☐

(B) Listen and match. 🎧 108

1 b

2 t

3 j

4 p

-en

-ed

-et

(C) Circle and write.

1

-en -et

2

-ed -et

3

-en -et

_____ _____ _____

Review 4

A Listen and number. 🎧 109

B Read and write the letters.

What do you see?

1 I see a truck. ☐

2 I see a train. ☐

3 I see a bike. ☐

4 I see a taxi. ☐

What do you want?

5 I want an apple. ☐

6 I want a carrot. ☐

7 I want a potato. ☐

8 I want an onion. ☐

Word List 1B

Unit 1 | I'm Happy

angry _____

bad _____

can _____

dad _____

fan _____

happy _____

hungry _____

pan _____

sad _____

scared _____

sick _____

sleepy _____

thirsty _____

Unit 2 | I Have a Dog

bat _____

cap _____

cat _____

dog _____

fish _____

hamster _____

hat _____

map _____

parrot _____

pig _____

rabbit _____

tap _____

turtle _____

Unit 3 | I Can Jump

big _____

climb _____

dance _____

fly _____

jump _____

mix _____

pig _____

run _____

sing _____

six _____

swim _____

walk _____

wig _____

Unit 4 | Touch Your Nose

arms _____

ears _____

eyes _____

feet _____

fin _____

fit _____

head _____

hit _____

legs _____

mouth _____

nose _____

pin _____

sit _____

win _____

Unit 5 It's Sunny

box _____

cloudy _____

cold _____

fox _____

hot _____

mop _____

pot _____

rainy _____

snowy _____

sunny _____

top _____

windy _____

Unit 6 Put on Your Skirt

cap _____

cut _____

dress _____

fun _____

hut _____

jacket _____

nut _____

pants _____

run _____

shorts _____

skirt _____

socks _____

sun _____

T-shirt _____

Unit 7 I See a Plane

bike _____

bug _____

bus _____

car _____

cub _____

cup _____

hug _____

plane _____

ship _____

taxi _____

train _____

truck _____

tub _____

up _____

Unit 8 I Want an Apple

apple _____

banana _____

bed _____

carrot _____

jet _____

kiwi _____

mango _____

onion _____

orange _____

pen _____

red _____

ten _____

wet _____

Unit 1   I'm Happy

Structure	Vocabulary		Phonics	Subject Link
I'm happy.	happy	sleepy	Short Vowel a	Science
	sad	hungry	sad, dad, bad	
	angry	thirsty	can, pan, fan	
	scared	sick		

Unit 2   I Have a Dog

Structure	Vocabulary		Phonics	Subject Link
I have a dog.	dog	fish	Short Vowel a	Math
	cat	parrot	cap, map, tap	
	rabbit	hamster	cat, bat, hat	
	pig	turtle		
Review 1				

Unit 3   I Can Jump

Structure	Vocabulary		Phonics	Subject Link
I can jump.	jump	swim	Short Vowel i	Sports
	sing	walk	pig, big, wig	
	climb	fly	six, mix, fix	
	run	dance		

Unit 4   Touch Your Nose

Structure	Vocabulary		Phonics	Subject Link
Touch your nose.	eyes	head	Short Vowel i	P.E.
	nose	arms	pin, fin, win	
	ears	legs	sit, hit, fit	
	mouth	feet		
Review 2				

Unit 5 It's Sunny

Structure	Vocabulary		Phonics	Subject Link
It's sunny.	sunny	cold	Short Vowel o	Science
	cloudy	rainy	hot, pot	
	windy	snowy	top, mop	
	hot		box, fox	

Unit 6 Put on Your Skirt

Structure	Vocabulary		Phonics	Subject Link
Put on your skirt.	dress	shorts	Short Vowel u	Art
	skirt	pants	run, sun, fun	
	jacket	T-shirt	nut, hut, cut	
	socks	cap		
Review 3				

Unit 7 I See a Plane

Structure	Vocabulary		Phonics	Subject Link
What do you see?	plane	train	Short Vowel u	History
I see a plane.	car	bike	bug, hug	
	taxi	bus	tub, cub	
	ship	truck	up, cup	

Unit 8 I Want an Apple

Structure	Vocabulary		Phonics	Subject Link
What do you want?	banana	mango	Short Vowel e	Science
I want an apple.	orange	carrot	bed, red	
I want a kiwi.	apple	potato	pen, ten	
	kiwi	onion	jet, wet	
Review 4				

Unit **1**

Unit **1**

Unit **2**

Unit **2**

Unit **1**

Unit **1**

Unit **2**

Unit **2**

Unit **1**

Unit **1**

Unit **2**

Unit **2**

Unit **1**

Unit **1**

Unit **2**

Unit **2**

Unit 1 **scared**	Unit 1 **sick**
Unit 2 **pig**	Unit 2 **turtle**
Unit 1 **angry**	Unit 1 **thirsty**
Unit 2 **rabbit**	Unit 2 **hamster**
Unit 1 **sad**	Unit 1 **hungry**
Unit 2 **cat**	Unit 2 **parrot**
Unit 1 **happy**	Unit 1 **sleepy**
Unit 2 **dog**	Unit 2 **fish**

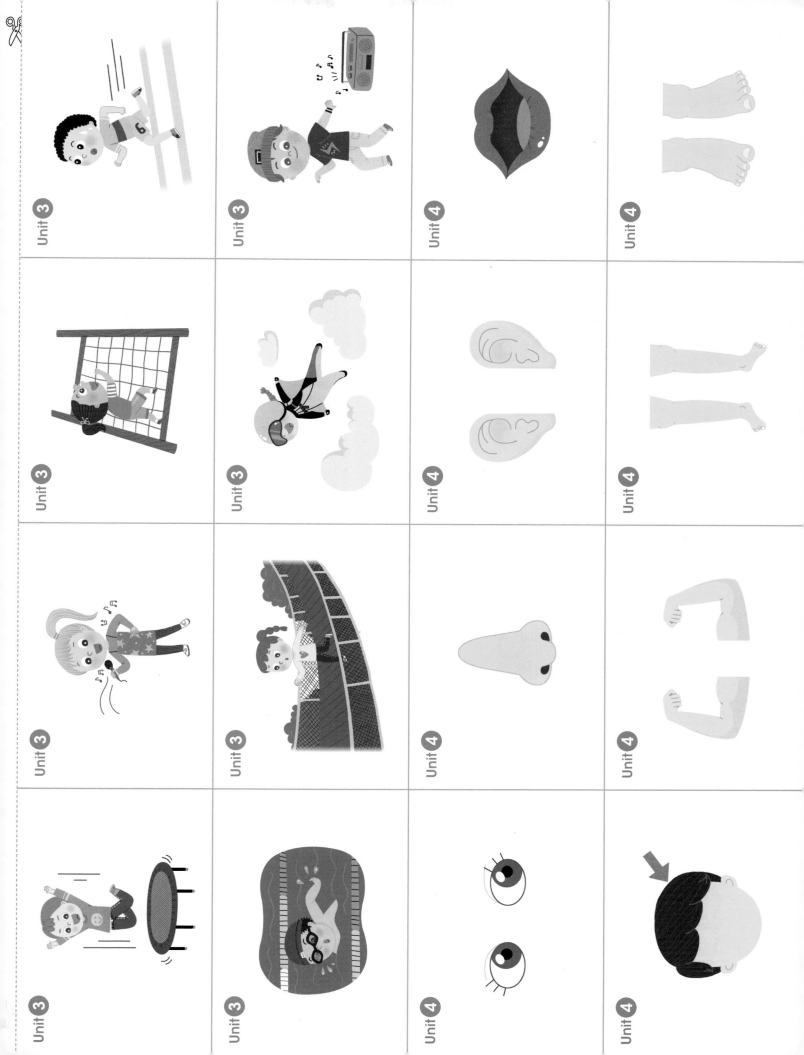

Unit 3

Unit 3

Unit 4

Unit 4

Unit 3 run	Unit 3 climb	Unit 3 sing	Unit 3 jump
Unit 3 dance	Unit 3 fly	Unit 3 walk	Unit 3 swim
Unit 4 mouth	Unit 4 ears	Unit 4 nose	Unit 4 eyes
Unit 4 feet	Unit 4 legs	Unit 4 arms	Unit 4 head

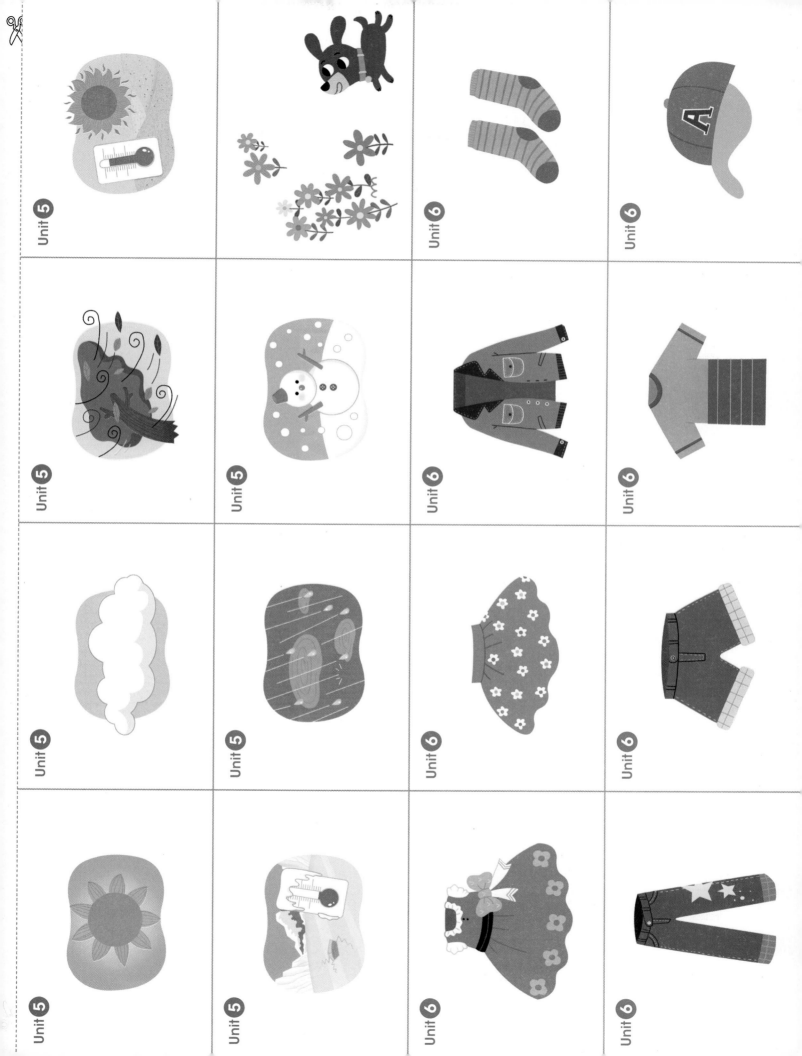

Unit 5

Unit 5

Unit 6

Unit 6

Unit 5

Unit 5

Unit 6

Unit 6

Unit 5

Unit 5

Unit 6

Unit 6

Unit 5

Unit 5

Unit 6

Unit 6

hot

socks

cap

windy

snowy

jacket

T-shirt

cloudy

rainy

skirt

shorts

sunny

cold

dress

pants

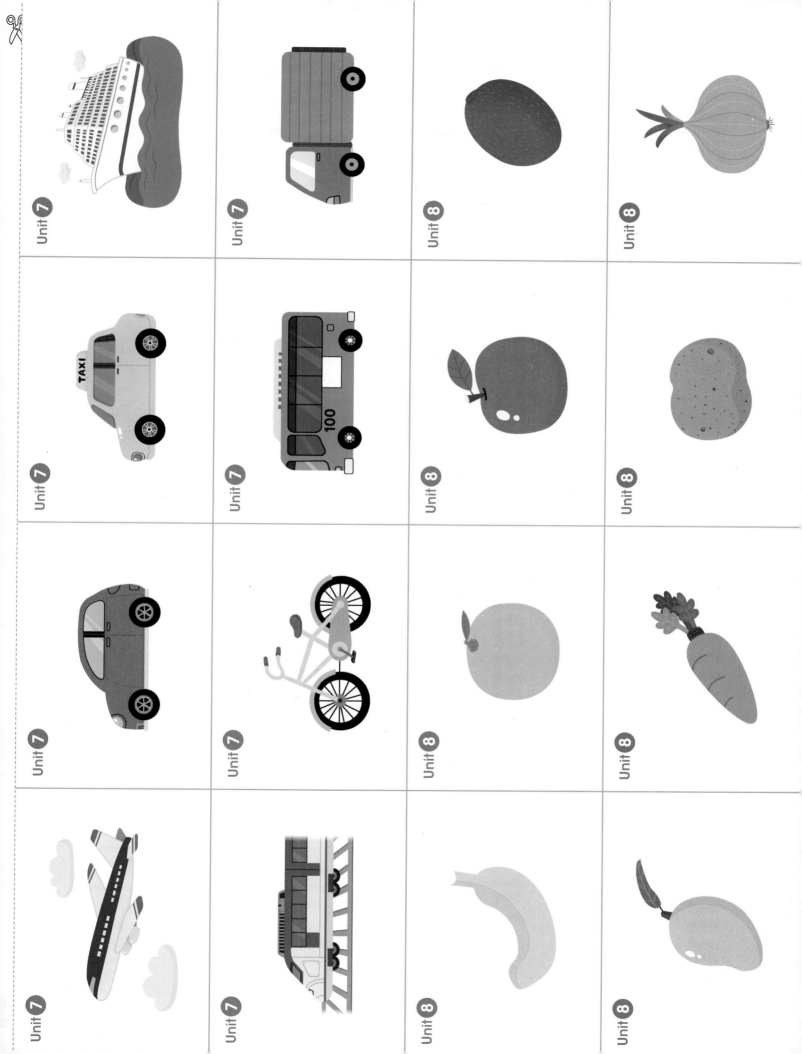

Unit 7

Unit 7

Unit 8

Unit 8

Unit 7

Unit 7

Unit 8

Unit 8

Unit 7

Unit 7

Unit 8

Unit 8

Unit 7

Unit 7

Unit 8

Unit 8

ship

truck

kiwi

onion

taxi

bus

apple

potato

car

bike

orange

carrot

plane

train

banana

mango

HOW MANY

DOGS ? CATS ?

DO YOU SEE?

Phonics

[11-12] Read and match.
철자를 읽어보고, 알맞은 그림과 연결하세요.

11 -ub •

- ⓐ
- ⓑ
- ⓒ **10**
- ⓓ

12 -et •

[13-14] Choose and write.
그림을 보고, 알맞은 단어를 골라 빈칸에 쓰세요.

13

taxi   bus   truck

_____

14

windy   snowy   cloudy

_____

15 Look and choose.
그림을 보고, 빈칸에 알맞은 말을 고르세요.

I want _____.

- ⓐ an orange
- ⓑ an onion
- ⓒ a carrot
- ⓓ a mango

[16-17] Read and choose.
문장을 읽고, 그림에 알맞은 것을 고르세요.

16

- ⓐ It's cloudy.
- ⓑ It's sunny.
- ⓒ It's cold.
- ⓓ It's raining.

17

- ⓐ Put on your socks.
- ⓑ Put on your skirt.
- ⓒ Put on your shorts.
- ⓓ Put on your dress.

18 Look and choose.
그림을 보고, 빈칸에 들어갈 알맞은 대답을 고르세요.

A: What do you see?
B: _____

- ⓐ It's a plane.
- ⓑ I see a bus.
- ⓒ I want a car.
- ⓓ I see a bike.

[19-20] Look and write.
그림을 보고, 빈칸에 알맞은 말을 쓰세요.

19

It's _____.

20

A: What do you want?
B: I want a _____.

Institute _____

Name _____

Score _____ /100

[1-3] Listen and choose.
잘 듣고, 그림에 알맞은 것을 고르세요.

1  ⓐ ⓑ ⓒ ⓓ

2  ⓐ ⓑ ⓒ ⓓ

3  ⓐ ⓑ ⓒ ⓓ

4 Listen and choose.
잘 듣고, 알맞은 그림을 고르세요.

ⓐ 　　ⓑ

ⓒ 　　ⓓ

Phonics

[5-6] Listen and choose.
잘 듣고, 알맞은 소리의 철자를 고르세요.

5 ⓐ -ox　　ⓑ -op　　ⓒ -ut　　ⓓ -ug

6 ⓐ -un　　ⓑ -ed　　ⓒ -ut　　ⓓ -ub

[7-8] Listen and choose.
잘 듣고, 빈칸에 들어갈 알맞은 단어를 고르세요.

7 It's _____.

ⓐ sunny　　　　ⓑ windy

ⓒ cloudy　　　　ⓓ cold

8 Put on your _____.

ⓐ skirt　　　　ⓑ cap

ⓒ jacket　　　　ⓓ dress

[9-10] Listen and choose.
대화를 잘 듣고, 빈칸에 알맞은 대답을 고르세요.

9

A: What do you see?

B: _____

ⓐ　　　　ⓑ　　　　ⓒ　　　　ⓓ

10

A: What do you want?

B: _____

ⓐ　　　　ⓑ　　　　ⓒ　　　　ⓓ

[11-12] Look and choose.
그림을 보고, 알맞게 짝지어진 것을 고르세요.

11 ⓐ -ix   ⓑ -ig

ⓒ  -ap   ⓓ  -ad

12 ⓐ  -ad   ⓑ  -ix

ⓒ  -an   ⓓ  -it

[13-14] Look and choose.
그림을 보고, 빈칸에 알맞은 것을 고르세요.

13

I _____ a dog.

ⓐ touch   ⓑ am
ⓒ can   ⓓ have

14

I can _____.

ⓐ walk   ⓑ fly
ⓒ jump   ⓓ dance

15 Unscramble.
단어를 배열하여 알맞은 문장을 만드세요.

hamster / have / a / I / .

···▶ _____

16 Read and mark ○ or ✗.
문장을 읽고, 그림과 일치하면 ○표, 일치하지 않으면 ✗표를 하세요.

Touch your mouth.

[17-18] Read and choose.
문장을 읽고, 그림에 알맞은 것을 고르세요.

17

ⓐ I'm sick.   ⓑ I'm scared.
ⓒ I'm angry.   ⓓ I'm full.

18

ⓐ I can climb.   ⓑ I can swim.
ⓒ I can run.   ⓓ I can jump.

[19-20] Look and write.
그림을 보고, 빈칸에 알맞은 말을 쓰세요.

19

Touch your _____.

20

I have a _____.

🎧 Midterm TEST 1B

Institute _____

Name _____

Score ___/100

[1-2] Listen and choose.
잘 듣고, 알맞은 그림을 고르세요.

1
ⓐ    ⓑ

ⓒ    ⓓ

2
ⓐ    ⓑ

ⓒ    ⓓ

3 Listen and choose.
잘 듣고, 그림에 알맞은 것을 고르세요.

   ⓐ   ⓑ   ⓒ   ⓓ

Phonics

[4-5] Listen and choose.
잘 듣고, 단어와 일치하는 소리의 철자를 고르세요.

4 ⓐ -ad   ⓑ -at
  ⓒ -an   ⓓ -it

5 ⓐ -ap   ⓑ -ig
  ⓒ -in   ⓓ -ap

6 Listen and choose.
잘 듣고, 문장에 알맞은 그림을 고르세요.

ⓐ    ⓑ

ⓒ    ⓓ

[7-8] Listen and choose.
잘 듣고, 빈칸에 알맞은 단어를 고르세요.

7

I'm _____.

ⓐ happy   ⓑ sad
ⓒ sick   ⓓ angry

8

I can _____.

ⓐ run   ⓑ climb
ⓒ dance   ⓓ swim

[9-10] Listen and choose.
잘 듣고, 그림에 알맞은 문장을 고르세요.

9    ⓐ   ⓑ   ⓒ   ⓓ

10    ⓐ   ⓑ   ⓒ   ⓓ

Let's Go · 1B

p. 4

p. 13

p. 15

p. 22

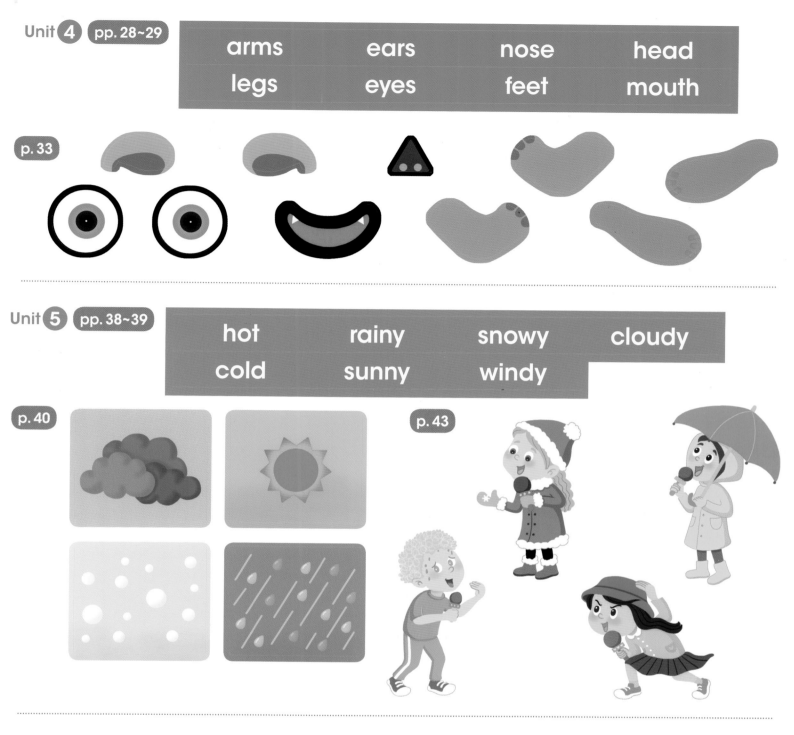

Unit 4 pp. 28~29

arms ears nose head
legs eyes feet mouth

p. 33

Unit 5 pp. 38~39

hot rainy snowy cloudy
cold sunny windy

p. 40

p. 43

Unit 6 pp. 46~47

cap dress pants jacket
skirt socks shorts T-shirt

p. 49

socks

shorts

cap

T-shirt

jacket

dress

p. 51

Unit **7** pp. 56~57

car	taxi	bike	truck
bus	ship	train	plane

p. 59

 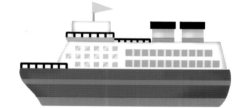 

Unit **8** pp. 64~65

a kiwi	an apple	a mango	an orange
a carrot	an onion	a potato	a banana

p. 69

2nd Edition

LET'S GO

to the English World

1B

Word Book
& Workbook

CHUNJAE EDUCATION, INC.

Word Book

Ⓐ Listen and trace. Then say. 🎧02

①  **angry**
화난

②  **thirsty**
목이 마른

③  **happy**
행복한

④  **hungry**
배고픈

⑤  **sad**
슬픈

⑥  **scared**
겁먹은, 무서워하는

⑦  **sick**
아픈

⑧  **sleepy**
졸린

 **I'm sad.** 나는 슬퍼.

 **I'm happy.** 나는 행복해.

B **Trace, write, and say.**

❶ 화난   angry

❷ 목이 마른   thirsty

❸ 행복한   happy

❹ 배고픈   hungry

❺ 슬픈   sad

❻ 겁먹은, 무서워하는   scared

❼ 아픈   sick

❽ 졸린   sleepy

I Have a Dog

Ⓐ Listen and trace. Then say. 🎧15

①  **dog**
개

②  **cat**
고양이

③  **rabbit**
토끼

④  **pig**
돼지

⑤  **fish**
물고기

⑥  **parrot**
앵무새

⑦  **hamster**
햄스터

⑧  **turtle**
바다거북

 **I have a cat.** 나는 고양이를 길러.

 I have a hamster. 나는 햄스터를 길러.

4

Ⓑ **Trace, write, and say.**

❶ 개   dog

❷ 고양이   cat

❸ 토끼   rabbit

❹ 돼지   pig

❺ 물고기   fish

❻ 앵무새   parrot

❼ 햄스터   hamster

❽ 바다거북   turtle

Ⓐ Listen and trace. Then say. 🎧29

①  **jump**
점프하다

②  **sing**
노래하다

③  **climb**
오르다

④  **run**
달리다

⑤  **swim**
수영하다

⑥  **walk**
걷다

⑦  **fly**
날다

⑧ **dance**
춤추다

 **I can** sing. 나는 노래할 수 있어.

 **I can** jump. 나는 점프할 수 있어.

B Trace, write, and say.

❶ 점프하다   jump

❷ 노래하다   sing

❸ 오르다   climb

❹ 달리다   run

❺ 수영하다   swim

❻ 걷다   walk

❼ 날다   fly

❽ 춤추다   dance

Ⓐ Listen and trace. Then say. 🎧42

①  **eyes**
(양쪽)눈

②  **nose**
코

③  **ears**
(양쪽)귀

④  **mouth**
입

⑤  **head**
머리

⑥  **arms**
(양쪽)팔

⑦  **legs**
(양쪽)다리

⑧  **feet**
(양쪽)발

 **Touch your** eyes. 네 눈을 만져 봐.

 **Touch your** nose. 네 코를 만져 봐.

B Trace, write, and say.

❶ (양쪽) 눈   eyes

❷ 코   nose

❸ (양쪽) 귀   ears

❹ 입   mouth

❺ 머리   head

❻ (양쪽) 팔   arms

❼ (양쪽) 다리   legs

❽ (양쪽) 발   feet

Ⓐ Listen and trace. Then say. 🎧56

①
sunny
화창한

②
cloudy
구름 낀, 흐린

③
windy
바람이 부는

④
hot
더운

⑤
cold
추운

⑥
rainy
비가 오는

⑦
snowy
눈 내리는

 **It's snowy.** 눈이 와.

 **It's sunny.** 화창해.

10

B Trace, write, and say.

① 화창한 sunny

② 구름 낀,
흐린 cloudy

③ 바람이
부는 windy

④ 더운 hot

⑤ 추운 cold

⑥ 비가 오는 rainy

⑦ 눈 내리는 snowy

Put on Your Skirt

Ⓐ Listen and trace. Then say. 🎧69

①  **dress**
드레스, 원피스

②  **skirt**
치마

③  **jacket**
재킷

④  **socks**
양말

⑤  **shorts**
반바지

⑥  **pants**
바지

⑦  **T-shirt**
티셔츠

⑧  **cap**
(앞에 챙 달린) 모자

 **Put on your cap.** 네 모자를 써.

 **Put on your T-shirt.** 네 티셔츠를 입어.

B Trace, write, and say.

❶ 드레스,
　 원피스　　dress

❷ 치마　　skirt

❸ 재킷　　jacket

❹ 양말　　socks

❺ 반바지　　shorts

❻ 바지　　pants

❼ 티셔츠　　T-shirt

❽ 모자　　cap

Ⓐ Listen and trace. Then say. 🎧83

①
plane
비행기

②
car
자동차

③
taxi
택시

④
ship
배

⑤
bike
자전거

⑥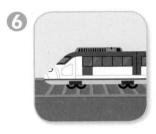
train
기차

⑦
bus
버스

⑧
truck
트럭

What do you see? 너는 무엇이 보이니?

I see a ship. 나는 배가 보여.

B Trace, write, and say.

❶ 비행기 plane

❷ 자동차 car

❸ 택시 taxi

❹ 배 ship

❺ 자전거 bike

❻ 기차 train

❼ 버스 bus

❽ 트럭 truck

Ⓐ Listen and trace. Then say. 🎧96

1
banana
바나나

2
orange
오렌지

3
apple
사과

4
kiwi
키위

5
mango
망고

6
carrot
당근

7
potato
감자

8
onion
양파

What do you want? 너는 무엇을 원하니?

I want an apple. 나는 사과를 원해.

B Trace, write, and say.

1 바나나   banana

2 오렌지   orange

3 사과   apple

4 키위   kiwi

5 망고   mango

6 당근   carrot

7 감자   potato

8 양파   onion

Workbook

I'm Happy

Learn

(A) Trace and match.

1 happy   2 sick   3 hungry   4 sad

5 scared   6 angry   7 sleepy   8 thirsty

B Circle and write.

1
sleepy
sad

I'm _____.

2
hungry
scared

I'm _____.

3
hungry
angry

I'm _____.

4
thirsty
sick

I'm _____.

5
happy
angry

I'm _____.

6
sad
thirsty

I'm _____.

7
scared
sick

I'm _____.

8
sleepy
happy

I'm _____.

Let's Talk

A Match and say.

1  I'm •

2 I'm •

3 I'm •

4 I'm •

• sick.

• happy.

• hungry.

• sad.

B Read and choose.

1 I'm sleepy.

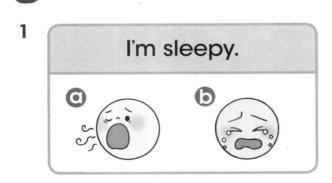

2 I'm thirsty.

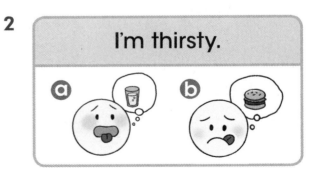

3 I'm scared.

4 I'm angry.

Words

Ⓐ Find, circle, and write.

s	i	c	k	s	o	h	a
a	d	h	u	r	s	a	h
d	i	s	l	e	e	p	y
s	c	a	r	e	d	p	t
t	h	i	r	s	t	y	k
f	t	a	n	g	r	y	s
h	u	n	g	r	y	d	j

1

h _____

2

s _____

3

a _____

4

s _____

5

s _____

6

h _____

7

t _____

8

s _____

Subject Link

A **Read and draw.**

1 **I'm angry.**

2 **I'm happy.**

3 **I'm hungry.**

4 **I'm sleepy.**

B **Follow and write.**

1 happy • ------ • I'm _____.

2 scared • ------ • I'm _____.

3 sick • ------ • I'm _____.

4 sad • ------ • I'm _____.

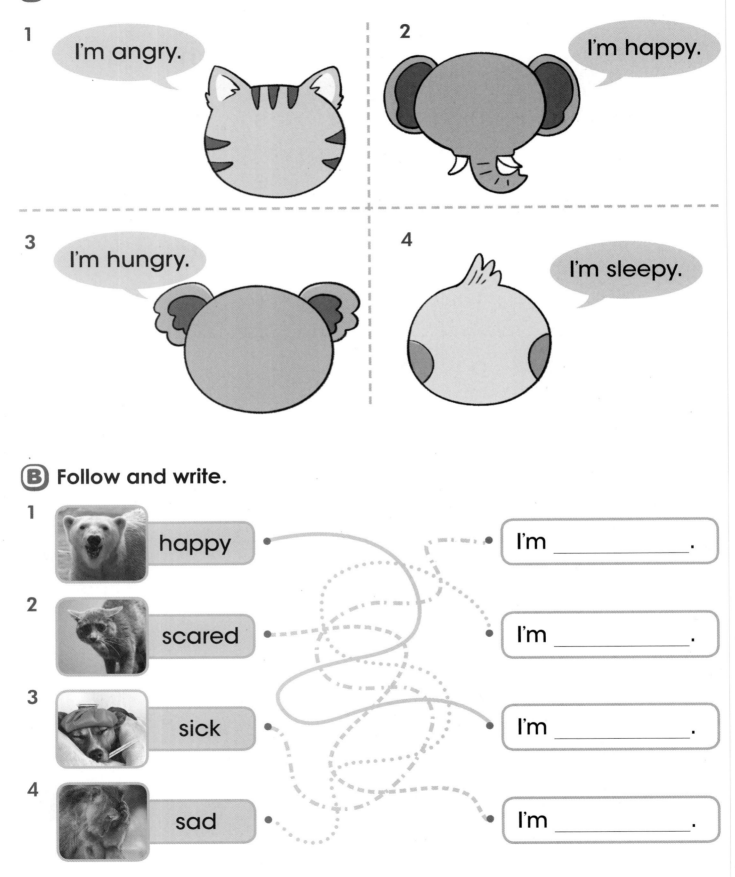

Phonics

A Circle and write.

1

-ad
-an

s _____

2

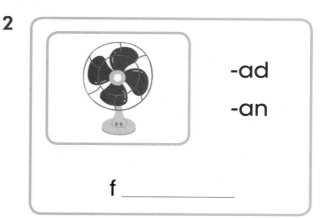

-ad
-an

f _____

3

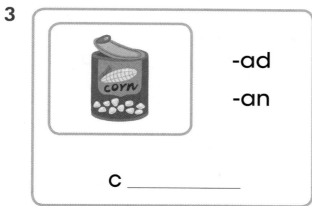

-ad
-an

c _____

4

-ad
-an

d _____

5

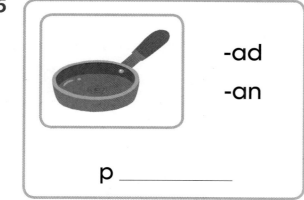

-ad
-an

p _____

6

-ad
-an

b _____

I Have a Dog

Learn

Ⓐ Circle and write.

1
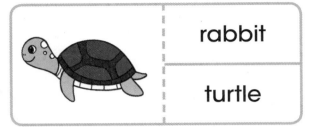

| rabbit |
| turtle |

_____

2
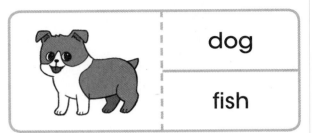

| dog |
| fish |

_____

3

| cat |
| pig |

_____

4

| turtle |
| rabbit |

_____

5

| parrot |
| pig |

_____

6
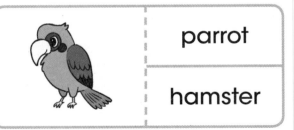

| parrot |
| hamster |

_____

7

| dog |
| hamster |

_____

8
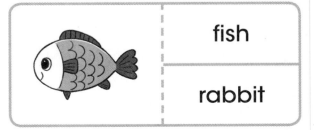

| fish |
| rabbit |

_____

B Trace and write the letters.

1 I have a cat. ☐

2 I have a parrot. ☐

3 I have a turtle. ☐

4 I have a hamster. ☐

5 I have a rabbit. ☐

6 I have a pig. ☐

7 I have a dog. ☐

8 I have a fish. ☐

Let's Talk

Follow and write.

1

2

I have a r_____.

I have a c_____.

3

4

I have a p_____.

I have a d_____.

5

6

I have a t_____.

I have a f_____.

I have a h_____.

7

8

I have a p_____.

28

Words

A Find, circle, and write.

catdogpigrabbitparrotturtlefishhamster

1  _____

2  _____

3  _____

4  _____

5  _____

6  _____

7  _____

8  _____

Subject Link

Ⓐ Read and mark O or X.

1

I have a dog. ☐

2

I have a pig. ☐

3

I have a turtle. ☐

4

I have a fish. ☐

Ⓑ Read and match.

1

 •  • • I have a dog.

2

• • • I have a rabbit.

3

 •  • • I have a fish.

4

•  • • I have a turtle.

Phonics

(A) Connect and write.

1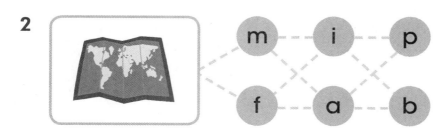

    c   a   t

    k   e   p

_____

2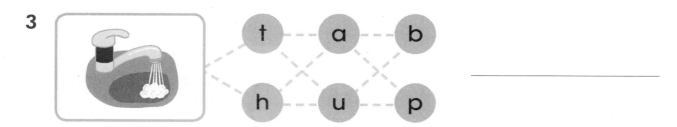

    m   i   p

    f   a   b

_____

3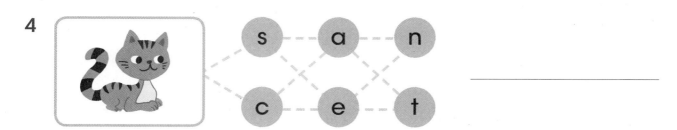

    t   a   b

    h   u   p

_____

4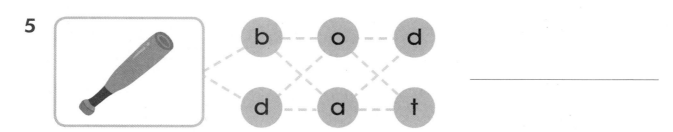

    s   a   n

    c   e   t

_____

5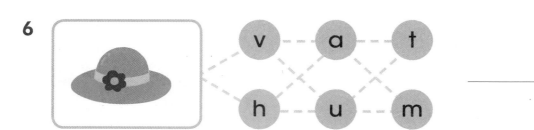

    b   o   d

    d   a   t

_____

6

    v   a   t

    h   u   m

_____

I Can Jump

Learn

Ⓐ Trace and circle.

1
jump

2
dance

3
swim

4
climb

5
run

6
fly

7
sing

8
walk

B Look and complete.

1

I can j ▢▢▢ .

2
I can s ▢▢▢ .

3
I can d ▢▢▢▢ .

4
I can r ▢▢ .

5
I can s ▢▢▢ .

6
I can f ▢▢ .

7

I can c ▢▢▢▢ .

8
I can w ▢▢▢ .

Let's Talk

1 I can jump.

2 I can dance.

3 I can fly.

4 I can climb.

5 I can sing.

6 I can run.

7 I can walk.

8 I can swim.

34

Words

A Unscramble and write.

1  p u j m

2  n r u

3  a d c e n

4  s g i n

5  b l m i c

6  y l f

7  k l w a

8  s i m w

Subject Link

Ⓐ Read and match.

1
| I can swim. |

2
| I can jump. |

3
| I can run. |

4
| I can dance. |

Ⓑ Look and write.

1  **2**  **3**  **4**

1 I can _____.

2 I can _____.

3 I can _____.

4 I can _____.

Phonics

(A) Which is different? Look and circle.

1 -ig

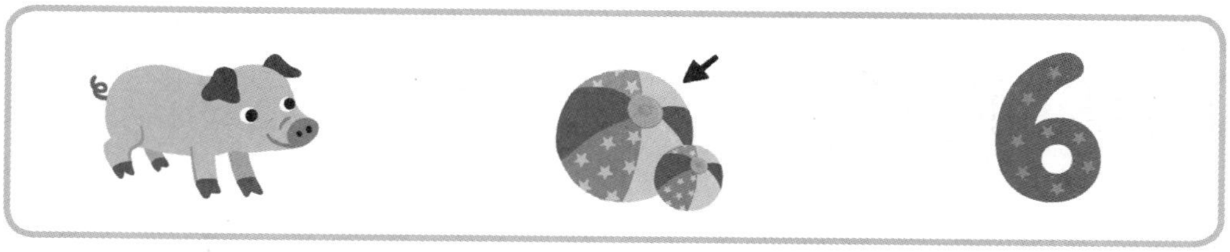

2 -ix

3 -ig

4 -ix

5 -ig

6 -ix

Learn

Ⓐ Look and write.

eyes	nose	ears	mouth
head	arms	legs	feet

1

2

3

4

5

6

7

8

B Unscramble and write.

1

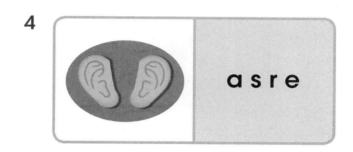

Touch your _____ .

2

Touch your _____ .

d e a h

e s e y

3

m a r s

Touch your _____ .

4

a s r e

Touch your _____ .

5

n e s o

Touch your _____ .

6

h o m t u

Touch your _____ .

7

e e f t

Touch your _____ .

8

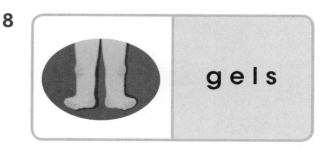

g e l s

Touch your _____ .

Let's Talk

A Read and check.

1

☐ Touch your nose.

☐ Touch your mouth.

2

☐ Touch your feet.

☐ Touch your legs.

3

☐ Touch your legs.

☐ Touch your arms.

4

☐ Touch your ears.

☐ Touch your eyes.

5

☐ Touch your mouth.

☐ Touch your head.

6

☐ Touch your arms.

☐ Touch your ears.

7

☐ Touch your head.

☐ Touch your nose.

8

☐ Touch your feet.

☐ Touch your eyes.

Words

A Color and write.

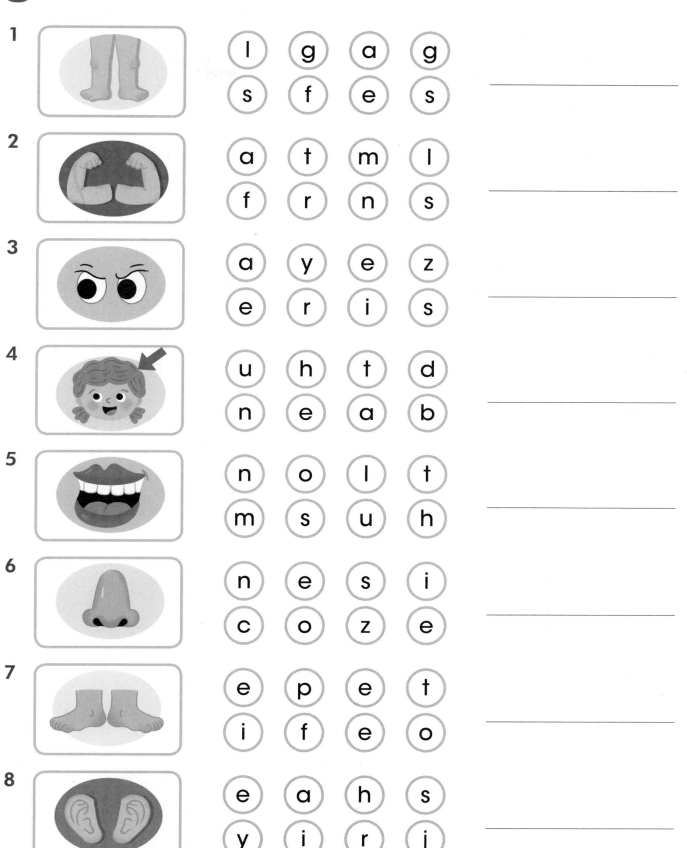

1   l g a g
    s f e s   _____

2   a t m l
    f r n s   _____

3   a y e z
    e r i s   _____

4   u h t d
    n e a b   _____

5   n o l t
    m s u h   _____

6   n e s i
    c o z e   _____

7   e p e t
    i f e o   _____

8   e a h s
    y i r j   _____

Subject Link

Ⓐ Read and mark O or X.

1

Touch your head. ☐

2

Touch your feet. ☐

3

Touch your legs. ☐

4

Touch your arms. ☐

Ⓑ Look and write.

1

Touch your _____.

2

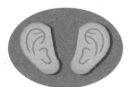

Touch your _____.

3

Touch your _____.

4

Touch your _____.

Phonics

(A) Write and say.

1
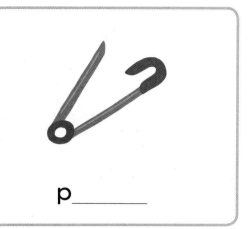
p_____

2

s_____

3
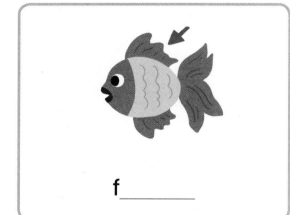
f_____

4
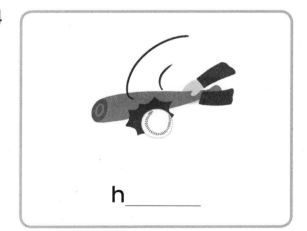
h_____

5
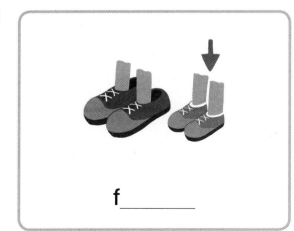
f_____

6

w_____

It's Sunny

Learn

A Trace and circle.

1 snowy

2 rainy

3 sunny

4 cold

5 cloudy

6 hot

7 windy

B Circle and write.

1

sunny

cloudy

It's _____.

2

hot

windy

It's _____.

3

cold

hot

It's _____.

4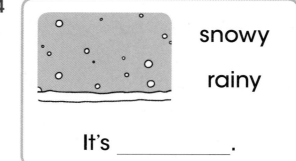

snowy

rainy

It's _____.

5

cloudy

windy

It's _____.

6

cold

sunny

It's _____.

7

hot

rainy

It's _____.

Let's Talk

A Look and match.

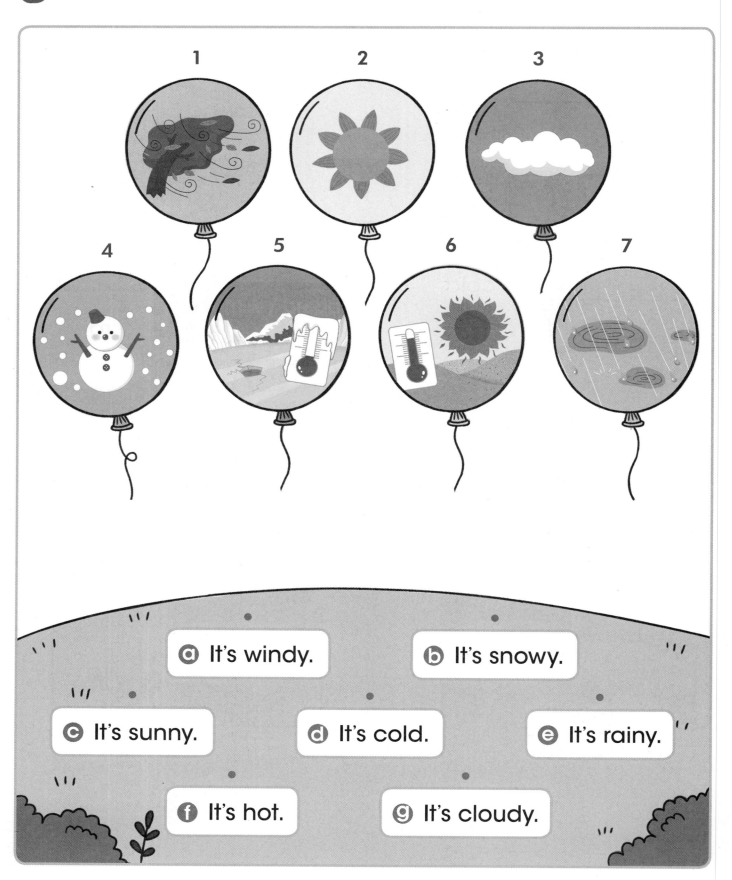

1

2

3

4

5

6

7

a It's windy.

b It's snowy.

c It's sunny.

d It's cold.

e It's rainy.

f It's hot.

g It's cloudy.

Words

A Complete and write.

1    cl___ ___dy   →

2    s___n___ ___   →

3 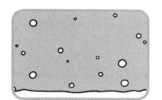   sn___ ___y   →

4    ___ai___y   →

5    w___ ___dy   →

6    c___ ___d   →

7 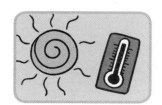   ___ ___t   →

Subject Link

Ⓐ Read and write the letters.

ⓐ ⓑ ⓒ ⓓ

1 | It's hot. | ☐
3 | It's snowy. | ☐

2 | It's windy. | ☐
4 | It's rainy. | ☐

Ⓑ Look and complete.

1
It's h_____.

2

It's c_____.

3
It's s_____.

4

It's c_____.

Phonics

A Circle and write.

1    hot   hit   hat

2    pop   pot   pan

3    top   tip   tap

4    map   mix   mop

5    bad   box   bat

6    fox   fit   fix

6 Put on Your Skirt

Learn

Ⓐ Trace and match.

1 jacket   2 shorts   3 dress   4 skirt

5 cap   6 socks   7 T-shirt   8 pants

B Look and write.

pants	jacket	cap	skirt
shorts	T-shirt	socks	dress

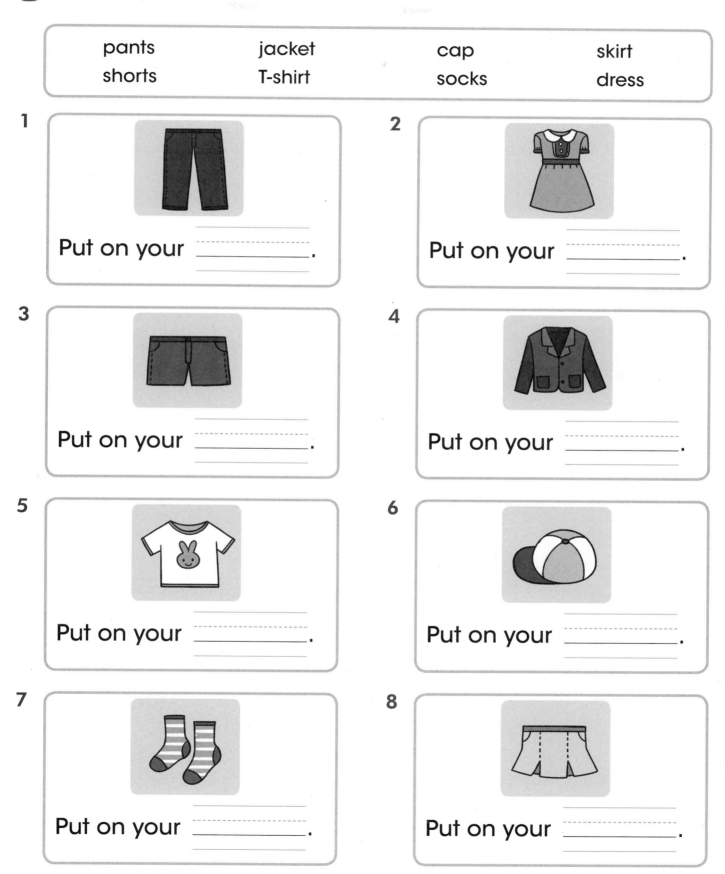

1 Put on your _____.

2 Put on your _____.

3 Put on your _____.

4 Put on your _____.

5 Put on your _____.

6 Put on your _____.

7 Put on your _____.

8 Put on your _____.

Let's Talk

Ⓐ Read and match.

1

- Put on your pants. -

- Put on your dress. -

2

3

- Put on your shorts. -

- Put on your jacket. -

4

5

- Put on your T-shirt. -

- Put on your cap. -

6

7

- Put on your socks. -

- Put on your skirt. -

8

Words

A Look and write.

1. T
2. c
3. d
4. p
5. s
6. s
7. j
8. s

| skirt | T-shirt | pants | cap |
| socks | shorts | jacket | dress |

Subject Link

Ⓐ Read and circle.

1  **2**  **3**  **4**

1 Put on your **pants** / **shorts** .

2 Put on your **socks** / **T-shirt** .

3 Put on your **jacket** / **cap** .

4 Put on your **cap** / **dress** .

Ⓑ Match and write.

1  •

2  •

3  •

• Put on your T-_____.

• Put on your s_____.

• Put on your c_____.

Phonics

(A) Circle and write.

1

-un
-ox

r_____

2

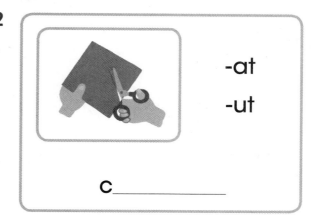

-at
-ut

c_____

3

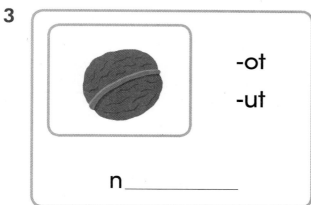

-ot
-ut

n_____

4

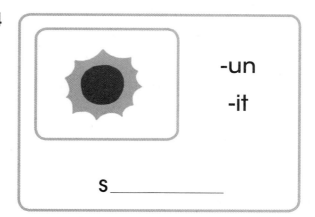

-un
-it

s_____

5

-un
-an

f_____

6

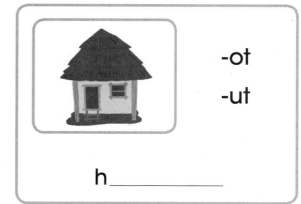

-ot
-ut

h_____

I See a Plane

Learn

Ⓐ Match and trace.

1

2

3

4

| bike | car | bus | train |

| truck | plane | ship | taxi |

5

6

7

8

B Circle and write.

1

trainbikeplane

I see a _____ .

2

carbustruck

I see a _____ .

3
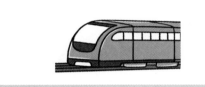

busshiptrain

I see a _____ .

4

shipbusplane

I see a _____ .

5

shipbustax

I see a _____ .

6

bikecarplane

I see a _____ .

7

taxitrucktrain

I see a _____ .

8

truckbikecar

I see a _____ .

Let's Talk

(A) Match and read.

1   I see   •   • a car.

2   I see   •   • a ship.

3   I see   •   • a taxi.

4   I see   •   • a bike.

5   I see   •   • a plane.

6   I see   •   • a truck.

(B) Read and check.

1

A: What do you see?

B: ☐ I see a plane.

    ☐ I see a train.

2

A: What do you see?

B: ☐ I see a bus.

    ☐ I see a truck.

Words

A Complete and write.

1  p___a___e → _____

2  ___ru___ ___ → _____

3  ___ ___ip → _____

4  t___x___ → _____

5 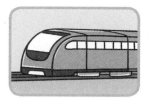 t___ai___ → _____

6  ___u___ → _____

7  ___ ___r → _____

8  ___ ___ke → _____

Subject Link

A Read and match.

1 [I see a plane.] •

2 [I see a train.] •

3 [I see a car.] •

4 [I see a ship.] •

B Look and write.

1

A: What do you see?

B: I see a _____ .

2

A: What do you see?

B: I see a _____ .

Phonics

Ⓐ Cross one out and write.

1

g ⊗

b u

bug
_____

2

p t

u

_____

3

h u

g t

_____

4

t n

u b

_____

5

c a

b u

_____

6

c u

p b

_____

I Want an Apple

Learn

A Circle and write.

1

banana
apple
_____

2

carrot
potato
_____

3

onion
kiwi
_____

4

mango
orange
_____

5

banana
mango
_____

6

carrot
potato
_____

7

kiwi
orange
_____

8

onion
apple
_____

B Trace and choose.

1
I want a **banana**.
a
b

2
I want an **apple**.
a
b

3
I want a **carrot**.
a
b

4
I want a **mango**.
a
b

5
I want a **kiwi**.
a
b

6
I want an **onion**.
a
b

7
I want an **orange**.
a
b

8
I want a **potato**.
a
b

Let's Talk

Ⓐ Read and match.

1 **I want a banana.** •
2 **I want an apple.** •
3 **I want a carrot.** •
4 **I want an onion.** •
5 **I want a mango.** •
6 **I want a kiwi.** •

Ⓑ Read and check.

1

A: What do you want?

B: ☐ I want a potato.

☐ I want a carrot.

2

A: What do you want?

B: ☐ I want an onion.

☐ I want an orange.

Words

Ⓐ Unscramble and write.

1

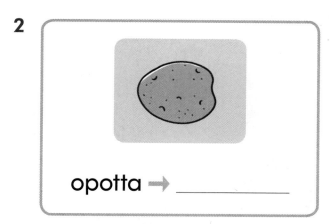

nabnaa ➡ _____

2

opotta ➡ _____

3

gmnao ➡ _____

4

lapep ➡ _____

5

tcraro ➡ _____

6

norega ➡ _____

7

oonni ➡ _____

8

iiwk ➡ _____

Subject Link

(A) Read and write the letters.

 a
 b
 c
 d

1 I want an apple. ☐

2 I want a kiwi. ☐

3 I want an onion. ☐

4 I want a carrot. ☐

(B) Look and write.

1

A: What do you want?

B: I want a m_____.

2

A: What do you want?

B: I want an o_____.

Phonics

Ⓐ Connect and write.

1. p   i   d
   b   e   n

   _____

2. r   r e   t
   빨강
   j   u   d

   _____

3. d   i   n
   p   e   g

   _____

4. t   a   m
   m   e   n

   _____

5. h   u   t
   j   e   n

   _____

6. f   e   t
   w   i   g

   _____